Circle the numbers 1–5 hidde

Count each group of fruits. Use the key to color each group.

Color the group of 1 yellow.
Color the group of 2 orange.
Color the group of 3 green.
Color the group of 4 blue.
Color the group of 5 red.

CD-104360

Draw a line through the numbers from 0 to 15 to help the detective find the footprint.

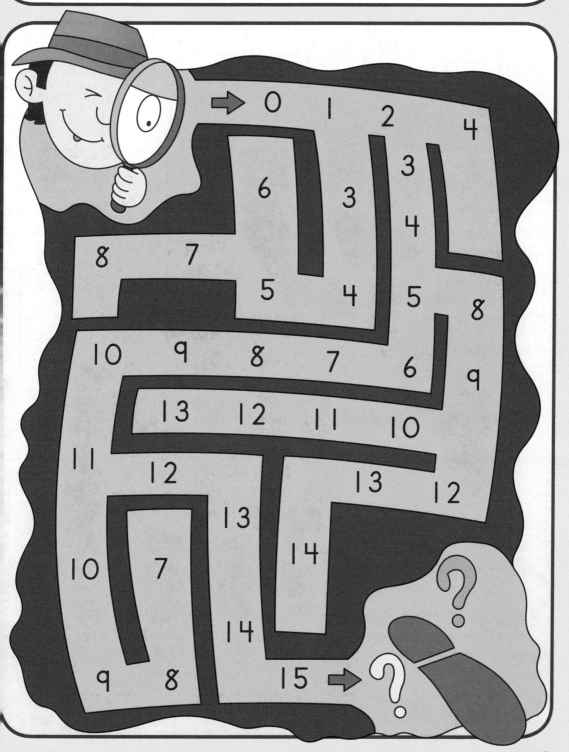

CD-104360 **3**

Match the numbers below to the number words in the code. Use the code to solve the riddle.

Why is 6 afraid of 7?

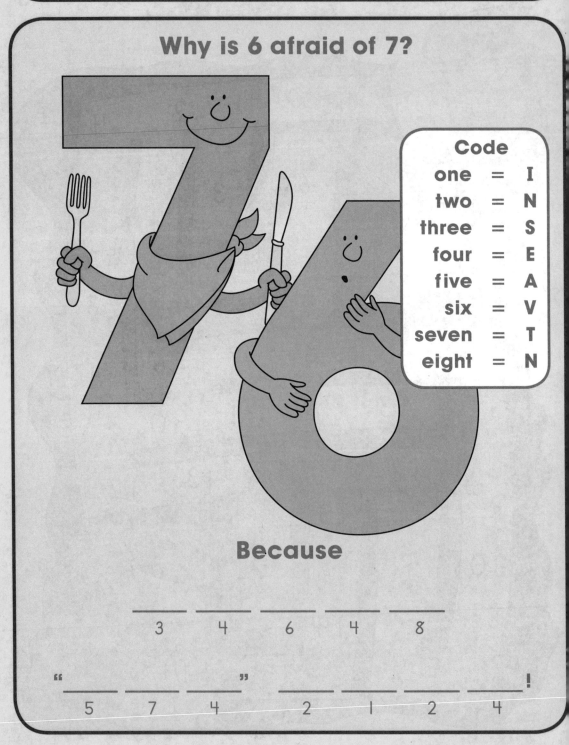

Code		
one	=	I
two	=	N
three	=	S
four	=	E
five	=	A
six	=	V
seven	=	T
eight	=	N

Because

___ ___ ___ ___ ___
3   4   6   4   8

" ___ ___ ___ " ___ ___ ___ ___ !
5 7 4   2 1 2 4

CD-104360

Unscramble each number word. Unscramble the circled letters to answer the question.

e g h i t   (e) i g h (t)

e t n   _ _ (_)

h t r e e   _ (_)(_) _ _

x s i   _ (_) _

i n n e   _ _ _ (_) _

o w t   (_) _ _

What number is three more than ten?

_ _ _ _ _ _ _ _

Write the correct number words to complete the crossword puzzle.

zero	one	two	three	four	five
six	seven	eight	nine	ten	

Across
3. 8
5. 4
6. 1
9. 7
11. 5

Down
1. 2
2. 0
4. 3
7. 9
8. 10
10. 6

Connect the dots from 1 to 30. Start at the ★.
Color the picture.

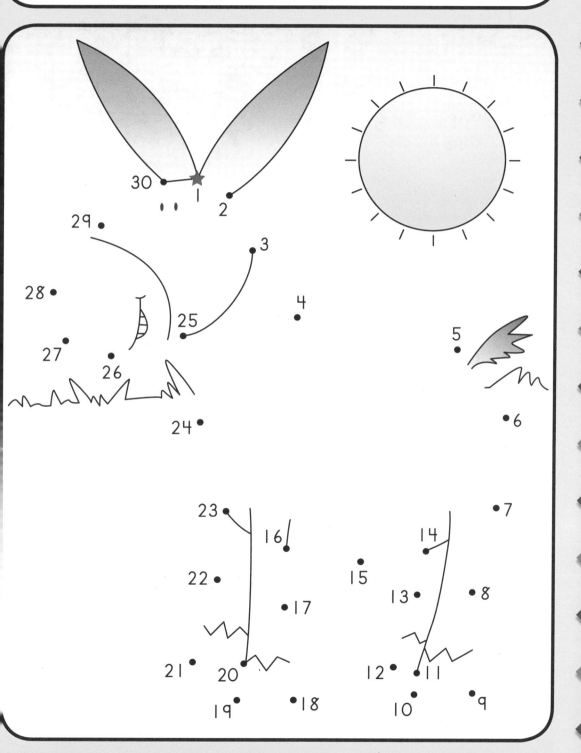

CD-104360

7

Circle the number words hidden in the puzzle. Words can be found across and down.

zero one two three
four five six seven
eight nine ten

```
z  e  r  o  n  h  e  f  v  s
y  s  r  d  d  b  a  o  n  e
h  t  h  r  e  e  f  m  v  v
g  y  o  o  f  o  u  r  k  e
q  n  p  e  n  f  p  c  n  n
d  v  s  i  y  i  w  a  m  f
q  x  g  g  b  v  n  i  n  e
d  h  e  h  v  e  j  t  p  r
t  w  o  t  l  i  o  e  f  g
s  i  x  m  m  f  y  n  a  m
```

Solve each problem. Use the key to color the picture.

4 = yellow   6 = blue   7 = green
8 = red   9 = purple

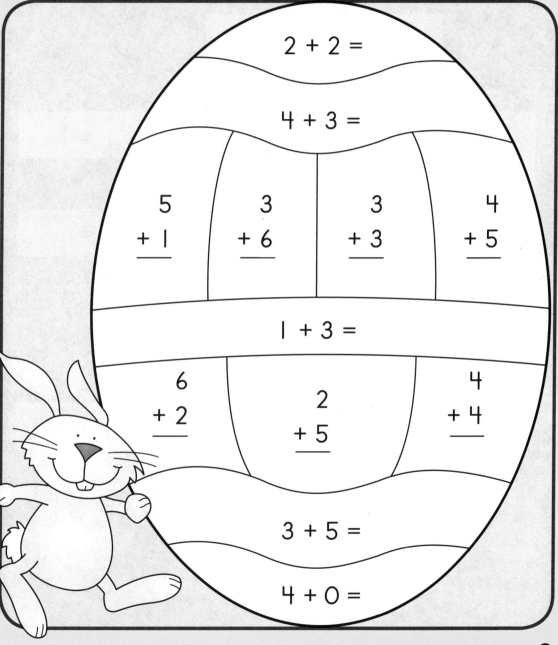

$2 + 2 =$

$4 + 3 =$

$\begin{array}{r} 5 \\ + 1 \\ \hline \end{array}$ $\begin{array}{r} 3 \\ + 6 \\ \hline \end{array}$ $\begin{array}{r} 3 \\ + 3 \\ \hline \end{array}$ $\begin{array}{r} 4 \\ + 5 \\ \hline \end{array}$

$1 + 3 =$

$\begin{array}{r} 6 \\ + 2 \\ \hline \end{array}$ $\begin{array}{r} 2 \\ + 5 \\ \hline \end{array}$ $\begin{array}{r} 4 \\ + 4 \\ \hline \end{array}$

$3 + 5 =$

$4 + 0 =$

Write the missing numbers to complete the puzzle.

1 2 3 4 5 6 7 8 9 10

	+	2	=	8				
		+		+				
2				1	+	6	=	
+		=		=				
3	+		=	4			+	1	=	
=		+					+	
		7						
		=					=	
					+	4	=	8

Circle the addition problems hidden in the puzzle. Write + and = between the numbers to complete each problem.

1	4	8	(3 + 4 = 7)			9	3
+							
2	5	4	2	1	9	4	2
=							
3	3	5	3	8	2	4	6
2	3	0	2	1	7	8	7
4	6	3	4	9	0	9	4
9	5	2	7	2	2	6	3
8	4	5	3	6	4	9	7

CD-104360

Solve each problem. Color the boxes that have sums of 10 to help the bird find his home.

	$\begin{array}{r} 3 \\ + 5 \\ \hline \end{array}$	$\begin{array}{r} 2 \\ + 1 \\ \hline \end{array}$	$\begin{array}{r} 0 \\ + 4 \\ \hline \end{array}$
$\begin{array}{r} 2 \\ + 8 \\ \hline \end{array}$	$\begin{array}{r} 6 \\ + 1 \\ \hline \end{array}$	$\begin{array}{r} 2 \\ + 2 \\ \hline \end{array}$	$\begin{array}{r} 4 \\ + 3 \\ \hline \end{array}$
$\begin{array}{r} 6 \\ + 4 \\ \hline \end{array}$	$\begin{array}{r} 7 \\ + 3 \\ \hline \end{array}$	$\begin{array}{r} 9 \\ + 1 \\ \hline \end{array}$	$\begin{array}{r} 7 \\ + 1 \\ \hline \end{array}$
$\begin{array}{r} 5 \\ + 2 \\ \hline \end{array}$	$\begin{array}{r} 2 \\ + 4 \\ \hline \end{array}$	$\begin{array}{r} 5 \\ + 5 \\ \hline \end{array}$	$\begin{array}{r} 3 \\ + 6 \\ \hline \end{array}$
$\begin{array}{r} 9 \\ + 0 \\ \hline \end{array}$	$\begin{array}{r} 5 \\ + 3 \\ \hline \end{array}$	$\begin{array}{r} 8 \\ + 2 \\ \hline \end{array}$	

 CD-104360

Solve each problem. Match the sums to the letters in the code. Use the code to solve the riddle.

Why did the dog visit the tree when he lost his voice?

$$\begin{array}{r} 6 \\ + 6 \\ \hline 12 \end{array}$$
Ⓗ

$$\begin{array}{r} 4 \\ + 4 \\ \hline \end{array}$$
◯

$$\begin{array}{r} 4 \\ + 7 \\ \hline \end{array}$$
◯

$$\begin{array}{r} 1 \\ + 7 \\ \hline \end{array}$$
◯

$$\begin{array}{r} 3 \\ + 5 \\ \hline \end{array}$$
◯

$$\begin{array}{r} 2 \\ + 7 \\ \hline \end{array}$$
◯

$$\begin{array}{r} 6 \\ + 2 \\ \hline \end{array}$$
◯

$$\begin{array}{r} 3 \\ + 6 \\ \hline \end{array}$$
◯

$$\begin{array}{r} 1 \\ + 1 \\ \hline \end{array}$$
◯

$$\begin{array}{r} 2 \\ + 1 \\ \hline \end{array}$$
◯

$$\begin{array}{r} 2 \\ + 2 \\ \hline \end{array}$$
◯

$$\begin{array}{r} 8 \\ + 0 \\ \hline \end{array}$$
◯

$$\begin{array}{r} 2 \\ + 4 \\ \hline \end{array}$$
◯

$$\begin{array}{r} 7 \\ + 3 \\ \hline \end{array}$$
◯

$$\begin{array}{r} 5 \\ + 2 \\ \hline \end{array}$$
◯

$$\begin{array}{r} 2 \\ + 3 \\ \hline \end{array}$$
◯ .

Code

2 = S
3 = O
4 = M
5 = K
6 = B
7 = R
8 = E
9 = D
10 = A
11 = N
12 = H

CD-104360

13

Connect the dots from 0 to 100. Count by 10s. Start at the ★. Color the picture.

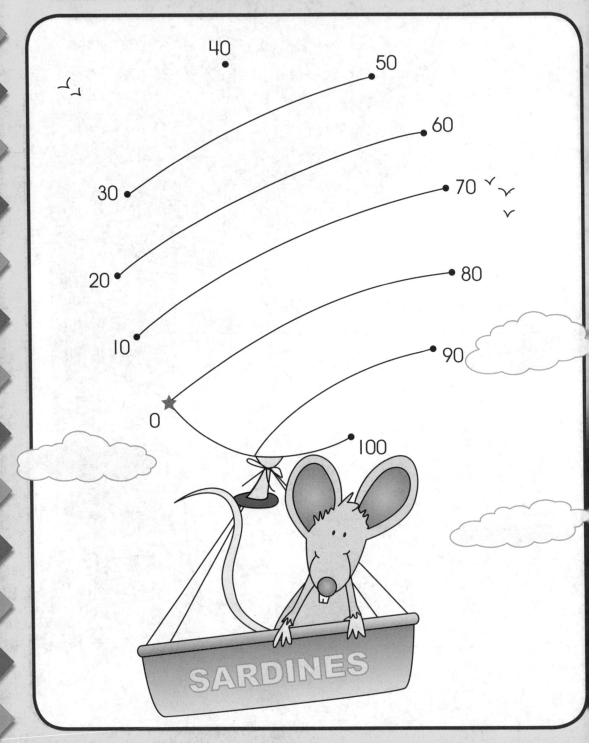

Solve each problem. Use the key to color each box and find the hidden symbol.

16 = blue   18 = red

9 + 9	10 + 8	10 + 6	18 + 0	7 3 + 8
2 9 + 7	6 5 + 7	8 + 8	3 9 + 6	4 8 + 6
3 7 + 6	1 9 + 6	5 5 + 6	10 5 + 1	2 8 + 6
1 9 + 8	2 7 + 9	5 9 + 2	5 7 + 6	9 6 + 3
10 + 8	8 4 + 6	9 + 7	2 8 + 8	10 1 + 7

CD-104360

15

Solve each problem. Color the sums in order on the paths to find which car finishes first.

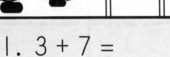

A

B

Start

10

4

13

9

1. 3 + 7 = ___   2. 4 + 9 = ___

3. 2 + 2 = ___   4. 6 + 3 = ___

5. 1 + 5 = ___   6. 8 + 8 = ___

7. 6 + 9 = ___   8. 4 + 4 = ___

9. 2 + 9 = ___   10. 5 + 7 = ___

11. 2 + 5 = ___   12. 7 + 7 = ___

13. 6 + 0 = ___   14. 2 + 1 = ___

15   6

8   16

Winner: _____

Finish

3   6   12

14   7   11

Solve each problem. Use the key to color the fish.

2 = red   4 = yellow   6 = blue   8 = green

$$\begin{array}{r} 6 \\ -\ 2 \\ \hline \end{array}$$

$$\begin{array}{r} 10 \\ -\ 4 \\ \hline \end{array}$$

$$\begin{array}{r} 9 \\ -\ 5 \\ \hline \end{array}$$

$$\begin{array}{r} 5 \\ -\ 3 \\ \hline \end{array}$$

$$\begin{array}{r} 12 \\ -\ 4 \\ \hline \end{array}$$

$$\begin{array}{r} 9 \\ -\ 1 \\ \hline \end{array}$$

$$\begin{array}{r} 12 \\ -\ 6 \\ \hline \end{array}$$

$$\begin{array}{r} 7 \\ -\ 5 \\ \hline \end{array}$$

Circle the subtraction problems hidden in the puzzle. Write – and = between the numbers to complete each problem.

18 – 9 = 9	10	4	9	8	3
4	6 (–)	2	7	2	11	6	5
12	3 (=)	8	3	2	7	4	9
2	4	1	15	8	7	6	2
7	6	14	5	9	4	8	0
1	13	2	9	6	7	3	16
0	5	9	3	0	9	5	8
12	8	7	10	6	4	1	8

Solve each problem. Color the boxes that have differences of 3 to help the chick find his mother.

	$\begin{array}{r} 10 \\ -\ 7 \\ \hline \end{array}$	$\begin{array}{r} 7 \\ -\ 4 \\ \hline \end{array}$	$\begin{array}{r} 10 \\ -\ 0 \\ \hline \end{array}$
$\begin{array}{r} 7 \\ -\ 6 \\ \hline \end{array}$	$\begin{array}{r} 12 \\ -\ 4 \\ \hline \end{array}$	$\begin{array}{r} 9 \\ -\ 6 \\ \hline \end{array}$	$\begin{array}{r} 18 \\ -\ 9 \\ \hline \end{array}$
$\begin{array}{r} 14 \\ -\ 6 \\ \hline \end{array}$	$\begin{array}{r} 11 \\ -\ 9 \\ \hline \end{array}$	$\begin{array}{r} 8 \\ -\ 5 \\ \hline \end{array}$	$\begin{array}{r} 9 \\ -\ 8 \\ \hline \end{array}$
$\begin{array}{r} 7 \\ -\ 1 \\ \hline \end{array}$	$\begin{array}{r} 6 \\ -\ 3 \\ \hline \end{array}$	$\begin{array}{r} 12 \\ -\ 9 \\ \hline \end{array}$	$\begin{array}{r} 9 \\ -\ 3 \\ \hline \end{array}$
	$\begin{array}{r} 11 \\ -\ 8 \\ \hline \end{array}$	$\begin{array}{r} 15 \\ -\ 8 \\ \hline \end{array}$	$\begin{array}{r} 16 \\ -\ 8 \\ \hline \end{array}$

 CD-104360

Write the missing numbers to complete the puzzle.

0   2   3   4   5   6   9

CD-104360

Solve each problem. Match the differences to the numbers below. Write the letters on the lines to solve the riddle.

15 Ⓡ − 7	14 Ⓜ − 8	9 Ⓥ − 7	10 Ⓞ − 9
8 Ⓐ − 5	7 Ⓘ − 3	12 Ⓔ − 7	11 Ⓣ − 4
17 Ⓢ − 8			

What kind of star is famous?

___   ___ ___ ___ ___ ___
  3   6   1   2   4   5

      ___ ___ ___ ___
       9   7   3   8

Solve each problem. Color the differences in order on the paths to find which rocket reaches the moon first.

1. $7 - 6 =$ _____

2. $5 - 2 =$ _____

3. $12 - 5 =$ _____

4. $8 - 6 =$ _____

5. $9 - 5 =$ _____

6. $14 - 6 =$ _____

7. $4 - 4 =$ _____

8. $11 - 6 =$ _____

9. $18 - 9 =$ _____

10. $9 - 3 =$ _____

Winner: _____

6	9
0	5
2	8
7	4
3	1

A

B

CD-104360

Solve each problem. Write the differences as number words. Unscramble the circled letters to solve the riddle.

1. $14 - 7 =$ __ __ __ (__) __

2. $12 - 3 =$ (__) __ __ __

3. $16 - 8 =$ __ (__) __ __

4. $9 - 5 =$ __ (__) __

5. $13 - 7 =$ (__) __ __

What do people make that you cannot see?

__ __ __ __ __ __

CD-104360   **23**

Solve each problem. Use the key to color the picture.

3 = green   4 = yellow   5 = orange
6 = blue   7 = brown

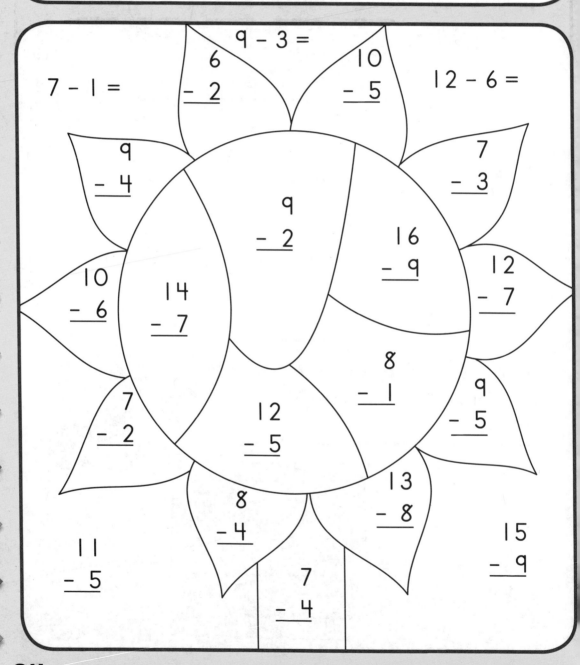

9 − 3 =

7 − 1 =

$$\begin{array}{r} 6 \\ -\ 2 \\ \hline \end{array}$$

$$\begin{array}{r} 10 \\ -\ 5 \\ \hline \end{array}$$

12 − 6 =

$$\begin{array}{r} 9 \\ -\ 4 \\ \hline \end{array}$$

$$\begin{array}{r} 7 \\ -\ 3 \\ \hline \end{array}$$

$$\begin{array}{r} 9 \\ -\ 2 \\ \hline \end{array}$$

$$\begin{array}{r} 16 \\ -\ 9 \\ \hline \end{array}$$

$$\begin{array}{r} 12 \\ -\ 7 \\ \hline \end{array}$$

$$\begin{array}{r} 10 \\ -\ 6 \\ \hline \end{array}$$

$$\begin{array}{r} 14 \\ -\ 7 \\ \hline \end{array}$$

$$\begin{array}{r} 8 \\ -\ 1 \\ \hline \end{array}$$

$$\begin{array}{r} 9 \\ -\ 5 \\ \hline \end{array}$$

$$\begin{array}{r} 7 \\ -\ 2 \\ \hline \end{array}$$

$$\begin{array}{r} 12 \\ -\ 5 \\ \hline \end{array}$$

$$\begin{array}{r} 13 \\ -\ 8 \\ \hline \end{array}$$

$$\begin{array}{r} 8 \\ -\ 4 \\ \hline \end{array}$$

$$\begin{array}{r} 15 \\ -\ 9 \\ \hline \end{array}$$

$$\begin{array}{r} 11 \\ -\ 5 \\ \hline \end{array}$$

$$\begin{array}{r} 7 \\ -\ 4 \\ \hline \end{array}$$

Use the key to color the shapes and find the hidden number. The picture will answer the question.

rectangle = green   hexagon = yellow

triangle = orange   square = brown

A farmer had 9 chickens. Four ran away. How many chickens does he have left?

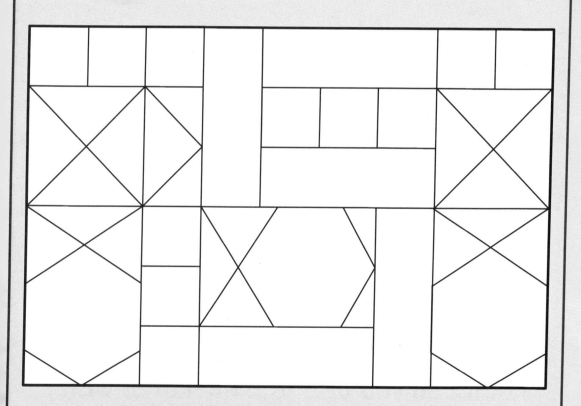

Answer:_____

CD-104360   **25**

Write the name of each figure. Unscramble the circled letters to solve the riddle.

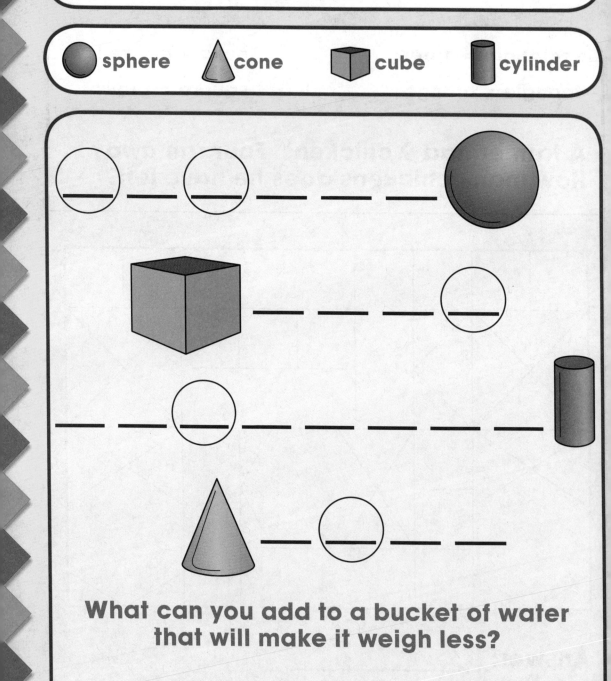

sphere   cone   cube   cylinder

$\bigcirc$ — $\bigcirc$ — — —

— — — — $\bigcirc$

— — $\bigcirc$ — — — — — —

— $\bigcirc$ — — — —

What can you add to a bucket of water that will make it weigh less?

— — — —

Use the key to color the figures.

= red

= orange

= blue

= green

Write the name of each shape to complete the crossword puzzle.

circle   square   sphere   cube
triangle   rectangle   cone   cylinder

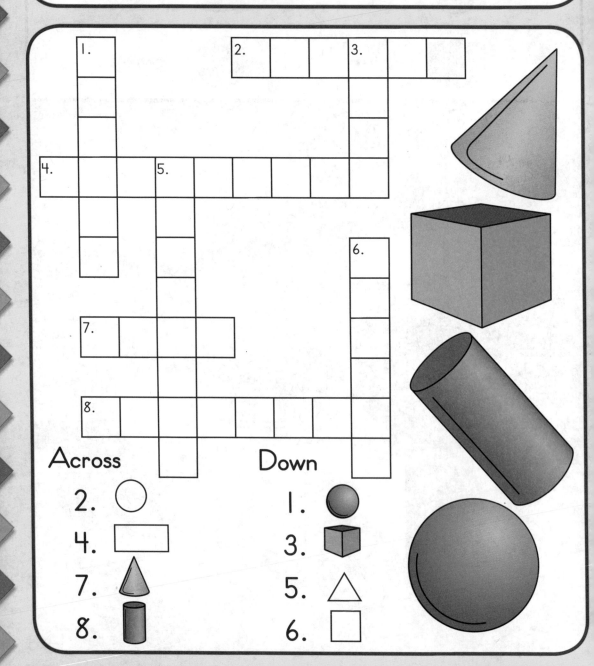

Across

2. ◯
4. ▭
7. ⬙ (cone)
8. (cylinder)

Down

1. (sphere)
3. (cube)
5. △
6. □

Finish the picture so that both halves match.

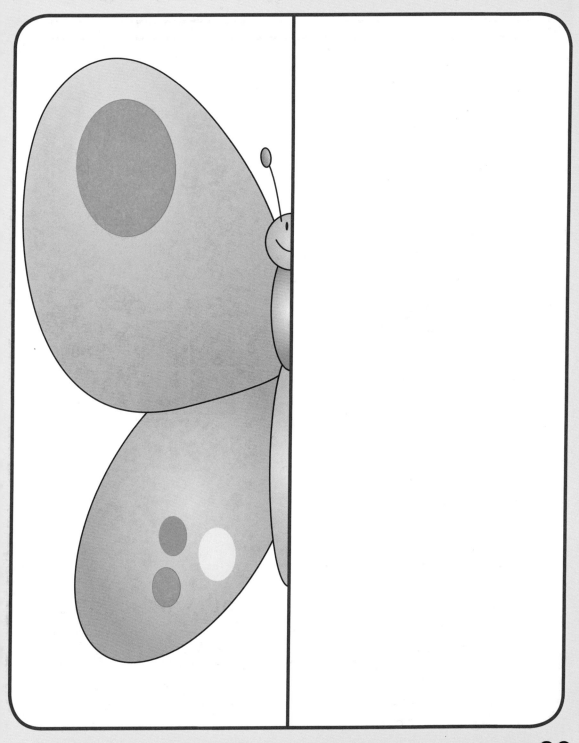

CD-104360

29

Write the number word to name how many equal parts are shown. The first one has been done for you. Unscramble the circled letters to solve the riddle.

(t) w (o)

What is the best thing to put into a muffin?

y _ _ _ _

_ _ _ _ _

Page 1

Page 2

The pictures should be colored as follows: banana–yellow, oranges–orange, pears–green, blueberries–blue, strawberries–red.

Page 3

The maze should follow the numbers 0–15.

Page 4

Because seven "ate" nine!

Page 5

From top to bottom: ten, three, six, nine, two; thirteen

Page 6

Page 7

The dots should be connected to form a donkey.

Page 8

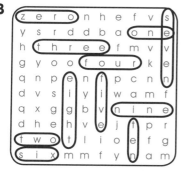

Page 9

From top to bottom and left to right: 4, 7, 6, 9, 6, 9, 4, 8, 7, 8, 8, 4

Page 10

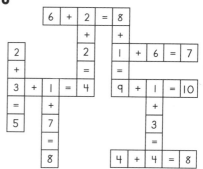

Page 11

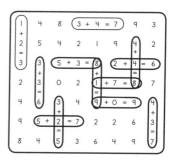

Page 12

Row 1: 8, 3, 4; Row 2: 10, 7, 4, 7; Row 3: 10, 10, 10, 8; Row 4: 7, 6, 10, 9; Row 5: 9, 8, 10; The boxes that have sums of 10 should be colored.

Page 13

Row 1: 8; Row 2: 11, 8, 8, 9, 8, 9; Row 3: 2, 3, 4, 8; Row 4: 6, 10, 7, 5; He needed some bark.

Page 14

The dots should be connected to form a balloon.

Page 15

Row 1: 18, 18, 16, 18, 18; Row 2: 18, 18, 16, 18, 18; Row 3: 16, 16, 16, 16, 16; Row 4: 18, 18, 16, 18, 18; Row 5: 18, 18, 16, 18, 18; The picture should show a + sign.

Page 16

1. 10; 2. 13; 3. 4; 4. 9; 5. 6; 6. 16;
7. 15; 8. 8; 9. 11; 10. 12; 11. 7; 12. 14;
13. 6; 14. 3; Car A wins.

Page 17

From left to right and top to bottom:
4, 6, 4, 2, 8, 8, 6, 2

Page 18

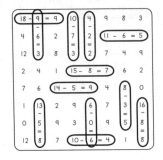

Page 19

Row 1: 3, 3, 10; Row 2: 1, 8, 3, 9;
Row 3: 8, 2, 3, 1; Row 4: 6, 3, 3,
6; Row 5: 3, 7, 8; The boxes with
differences of 3 should be colored.

Page 20

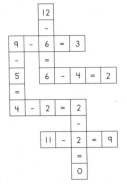

Page 21

Row 1: 8, 6, 2, 1; Row 2: 3, 4, 5, 7;
Row 3: 9; A movie star

Page 22

1. 1; 2. 3; 3. 7; 4. 2; 5. 4; 6. 8; 7. 0;
8. 5; 9. 9; 10. 6; Rocket B reaches
the moon first.

Page 23

1. seven; 2. nine; 3. eight; 4. four;
5. six; Noise

Page 24

From left to right and top to bottom:
6, 4, 6, 5, 6, 5, 7, 7, 4, 4, 7, 5, 5, 7, 7,
4, 6, 4, 5, 6, 3. The picture should
show a flower.

Page 25

The picture should show a 5.;
Five chickens are left.

Page 26

From top to bottom: sphere, cube,
cylinder, cone; Holes

Page 27

Page 28

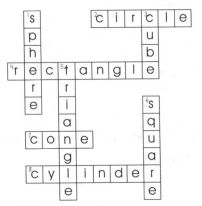

Page 29

Check that the picture is complete.

Page 30

From top to bottom: two, three, five,
four, eight; your teeth

Page 31
Check that there are two balloons in each color.

Page 32
The maze should follow the closed figures from start to finish.

Page 33
The dots should be connected to form a kangaroo.

Page 34
There are 8 single apples, 3 bushels of apples, and 38 apples in all.

Page 35
The mystery number is 111.

Page 36
The correct path follows the numbers 2, 4, 6, 8, 10, 12, 14, 16, 18, and 20.

Page 37
The dots should be connected to form a turtle.

Page 38
Check that the roller coaster cars are colored according to the key.

Page 39
These matches should be made:
1st–first; 2nd–second; 3rd–third; 4th–fourth; 5th–fifth; 6th–sixth; 7th–seventh; 8th–eighth; 9th–ninth; 10th–tenth.

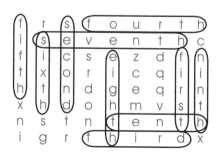

Page 40
The path should follow: 1, 5, 15, 17, 21, 24, 35, 40, 42, 44, 46, 47, 51, 55, 58, 59, 61, 63, 65, 67, 69, 70, 75, 82, 90, 95.

Page 41
The path should follow the numbers 30–1 backward.

Page 42

```
10  12  13  49  55  46  (13)
 9 (21  22  23) 15  19  (14
(44) 31  35 (16  17  18)(15)
(45) 11  12  14 (97  98  99)
(46) 60 (62) 69  72  74  75
 49  50 (63) 80 (87 (88) 89)
 44  52 (64) 65  68 (89)(77)
(50  51  52) 66  64 (90)(78)
 51  55  43  70  66  95 (79)
```

Page 43
From top to bottom: Folder 1: 8, 6, 11, 3, 14; Folder 2: 6, 4, 8, 2, 10; Folder 3: 2, 4, 1, 5, 6

Page 44
From top to bottom: Folder 1: 6, 1, 7, 2, 5; Folder 2: 9, 4, 6, 1, 5; Folder 3: 3, 2, 1, 0, 1

Page 45
The path should follow: 9 > 5, 14 > 12, 25 > 17, 35 < 40, 55 > 46, 70 > 68, 80 > 75, 87 < 91, 95 > 93.

Page 46
The dots should be connected to form a clock. Check that the correct numbers are written in the clock. Check that the clock shows 8:00.

Page 47
10:00 = blue; 1:30 = red; 7:30 = green; 3:00 = yellow.

Page 48

The leaves and tree should be labeled 2:00, 2:30, 3:00, 3:30, 4:00, 4:30; The caterpillar reaches the tree at 4:30.

Page 49

Page 50

Page 51

The following boxes should be colored: TV, car, elephant, tree, truck, bed, piano, treasure chest

Page 52

1. glass; 2. pail; 3. tub; 4. ocean; Vegetables

Page 53

From left to right and top to bottom: 58, 26, 92, 87, 99, 38, 79, 86, 49, 97, 27, 59, 67, 69, 73, 66; More red boxes are colored.

Page 54

1. 37; 2. 29; 3. 58; 4. 100; 5. 47; 6. 39; 7. 89; 8. 58; 9. 38; 10. 79; Sub B reaches the surface first.

Page 55

1. 57; 2. 60; 3. 99; 4. 79; 5. 19; 6. 16; 7. 59; 8. 67; 9. 17; 10. 48; Bee B reaches the flowers first.

Page 56

From left to right and top to bottom: 83, 28, 66, 97, 74, 49, 68, 98; A mushroom

Page 57

The picture should show a sand castle.

Page 58

From left to right and top to bottom: 60, 76, 63, 31, 11, 60, 72, 57, 30, 62, 5, 31, 34, 61, 51, 83. Check that the spaces are colored according to the directions.

Page 59

From left to right and top to bottom: 72, 11, 23, 54, 12, 41, 30, 13; Tic-tac-toe is formed diagonally through 23, 41, 13.

Page 60

From left to right and top to bottom: 51, 64, 35, 4, 31, 30; A fence

Help the man divide his six balloons equally among the three children. Color the balloons pink, yellow, and orange to show the equal sets.

Draw a line through the path that has closed figures to help the scientist find the robot.

Examples of closed figures =

Examples of open figures =

Connect the dots from 25 to 55. Start at the ★.
Color the picture.

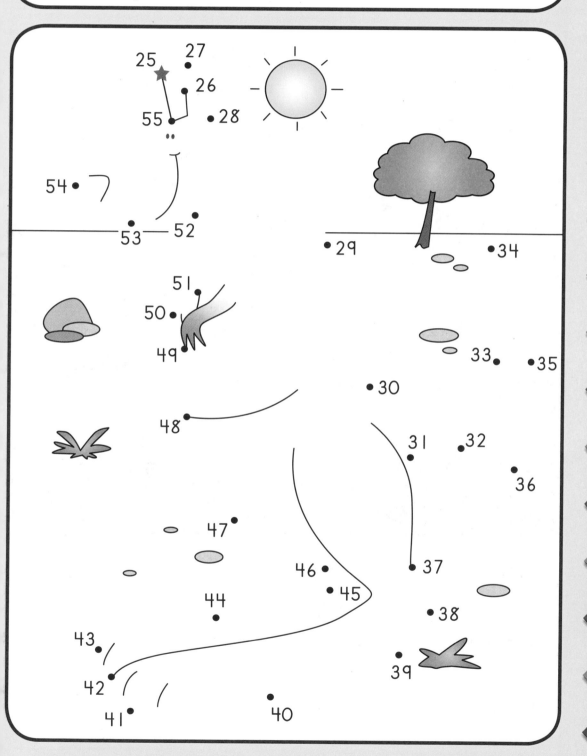

CD-104360

33

Add the apples to tell how many in all.

= 1 apple

= 10 apples

I found _____ .

I found _____ .

I found _____ apples in all.

CD-104360

Color the boxes that have numbers ending in **0**, **2**, or **5** to find the mystery number.

What number am I?
I am a number with 3 digits. I am greater than 100 but less than 200.

1	2	3	4	5	6	7	8	9	10
11	12	13	14	15	16	17	18	19	20
21	22	23	24	25	26	27	28	29	30
31	32	33	34	35	36	37	38	39	40
41	42	43	44	45	46	47	48	49	50
51	52	53	54	55	56	57	58	59	60
61	62	63	64	65	66	67	68	69	70
71	72	73	74	75	76	77	78	79	80
81	82	83	84	85	86	87	88	89	90
91	92	93	94	95	96	97	98	99	100

The mystery number is _____.

Count by 2s to help the frog reach the lily pad. Color the rocks that show the correct path.

CD-104360 © Carson-Dellosa

Connect the dots from 5 to 100. Count by 5s. Start at the ★.

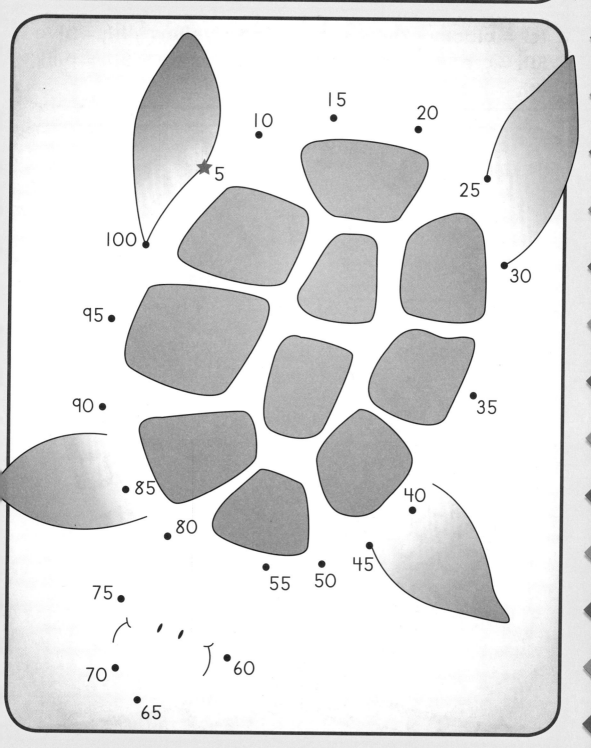

Use the key to color the roller coaster cars. The rocket is the **1st** car.

1st = black   2nd = red   3rd = yellow   4th = blue
5th = green   6th = purple   7th = white   8th = pink
9th = brown   10th = orange

CD-104360

Draw a line to connect each ordinal number to the correct ordinal number word. Circle the ordinal number words hidden in the puzzle.

1st	tenth
2nd	fifth
3rd	third
4th	ninth
5th	sixth
6th	second
7th	first
8th	seventh
9th	fourth
10th	eighth

```
f  r  s  f  o  u  r  t  h
i  s  e  v  e  n  t  h  c
f  i  c  s  e  z  d  f  n
t  x  o  r  i  c  q  i  i
h  t  n  d  g  e  q  r  n
x  h  d  o  h  m  v  s  t
n  s  t  n  t  e  n  t  h
i  g  r  t  h  i  r  d  x
```

CD-104360

39

Draw a line through the numbers in order from least to greatest to help the goose find her goslings.

CD-104360 © Carson-Dellosa

Color the boxes that show 1 less than the previous number. Start at 30 and finish at 1.

Start	30	29	26	17	16	13	10
29	25	28	3	6	9	12	11
9	14	27	26	25	24	13	15
12	13	30	29	20	23	27	28
11	9	7	20	21	22	24	17
13	14	15	19	22	5	4	3
15	16	17	18	23	6	9	2
14	10	11	14	8	7	8	1
13	12	11	10	9	11	10	Finish

CD-104360

41

Circle the sets of three numbers that are shown in order. The sets can be found across and down. The first one has been done for you.

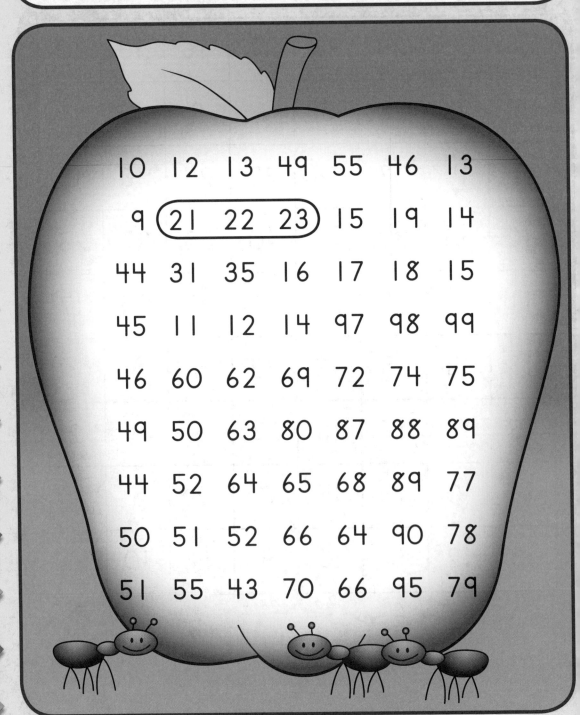

10	12	13	49	55	46	13
9	21	22	23	15	19	14
44	31	35	16	17	18	15
45	11	12	14	97	98	99
46	60	62	69	72	74	75
49	50	63	80	87	88	89
44	52	64	65	68	89	77
50	51	52	66	64	90	78
51	55	43	70	66	95	79

CD-104360

© Carson-Dellosa

Add across and down to find the secret number.

Add ➡

Add ⬇

7	1	
4	2	
		◯

Add ➡

Add ⬇

5	1	
3	1	
		◯

Add ➡

Add ⬇

1	1	
0	4	
		◯

CD-104360

43

Subtract across and down to find the secret number.

Subtract ➡

Subtract ⬇

10	4	
3	2	
		◯

Subtract ➡

Subtract ⬇

12	3	
6	2	
		◯

Subtract ➡

Subtract ⬇

8	5	
7	5	
		◯

CD-104360

Draw a line through the correct comparisons to help the alien reach the planet.

< = less than   **>** = greater than

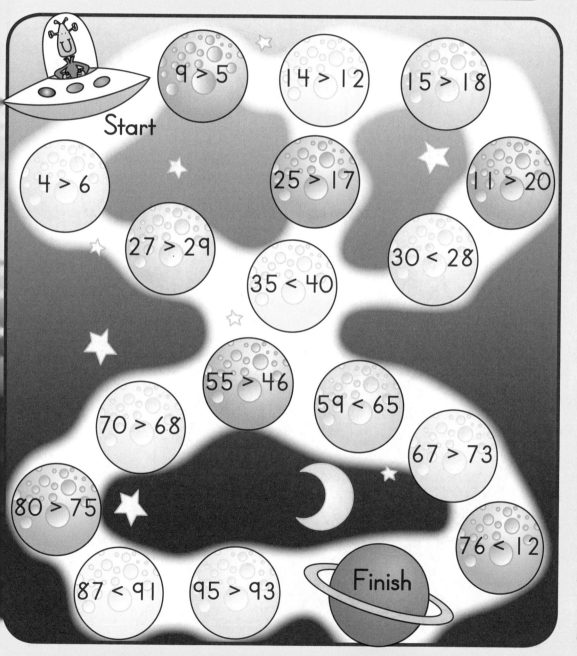

Start

9 > 5

14 > 12

15 > 18

4 > 6

25 > 17

11 > 20

27 > 29

30 < 28

35 < 40

55 > 46

59 < 65

70 > 68

67 > 73

80 > 75

76 < 12

87 < 91

95 > 93

Finish

CD-104360

45

Connect the dots from 10 to 100. Count by 10s. Start at the ★. Write the numbers 1–12 on the clock. Then, draw hands on the clock to show 8:00.

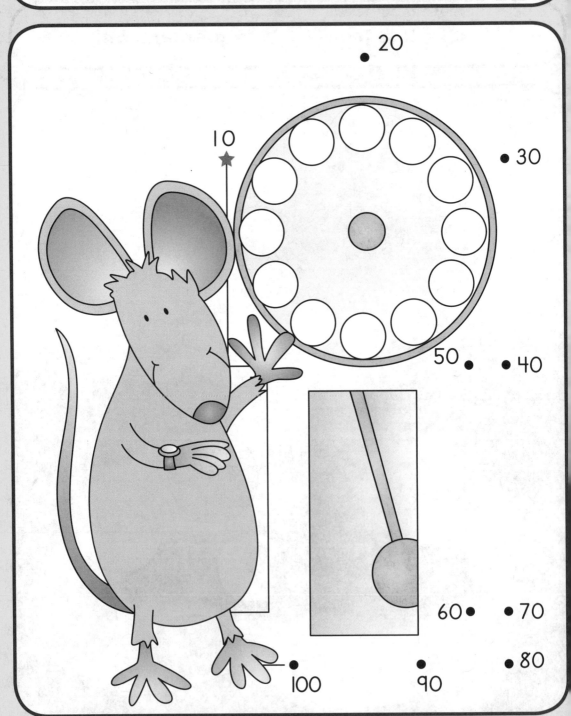

20

10

30

50 · 40

60· ·70

·80

100 90

Color the analog clocks as shown. Then, color the digital clocks with matching times the same colors.

= yellow

= blue

= red

= green

It takes 30 minutes for the caterpillar to crawl to each new leaf. Write the time that the caterpillar will reach each leaf. Then, answer the question.

1:30

___:___

___:___

___:___

___:___

___:___

___:___

What time will the caterpillar reach the tree?

_____

CD-104360

Circle the days of the week hidden in the puzzle. Words can be found across and down.

SUNDAY   MONDAY   TUESDAY

WEDNESDAY   THURSDAY   FRIDAY

SATURDAY

```
V S U N D A Y S Q T P C
C H Z E F G E M U G M D
R M I M I Z R I P S X W
P V W E D N E S D A Y V
P V V F J F J D W T Z J
F T W T K R P G R U W T
O V B P Y I V K Y R Z U
A N B W X D D P M D K E
T M O N D A Y V J A C S
B Y K P Y Y Y I R Y G D
I H I U E D P V Y D V A
T H U R S D A Y O E C Y
```

Find and circle 10 pencils hidden in the picture.

CD-104360

Help the horse find the barn. Color the boxes that have objects that weigh more than a backpack.

Compare each pair of objects. Write the name of the object that holds more water. Unscramble the circled letters to solve the riddle.

1. glass or spoon?

◯ ◯ ◯ __ __ __

2. cups or pail?

__ __ __ ◯ __

3. pot or tub?

◯ ◯ __ __

4. river or ocean?

__ __ ◯ __ __

What kind of tables do people eat?

v __ __ __ e __ __ __ __ __ __ e __

Solve each problem. Color the boxes that have sums greater than 50 red. Color the boxes that have sums less than 50 blue.

22 +36	15 +11	72 +20	44 +43
91 + 8	15 +23	63 +16	65 +21
18 +31	84 +13	14 +13	29 +30
55 +12	49 +20	63 +10	22 +44

Which do you have more of?

red boxes   blue boxes

 CD-104360

Solve each problem. Color the sums in order on the paths to find which sub reaches the surface first.

1. $\begin{array}{r} 14 \\ + 23 \\ \hline \end{array}$

2. $\begin{array}{r} 19 \\ + 10 \\ \hline \end{array}$

3. $\begin{array}{r} 45 \\ + 13 \\ \hline \end{array}$

4. $\begin{array}{r} 92 \\ + 8 \\ \hline \end{array}$

5. $\begin{array}{r} 16 \\ + 31 \\ \hline \end{array}$

6. $\begin{array}{r} 27 \\ + 12 \\ \hline \end{array}$

7. $\begin{array}{r} 67 \\ + 22 \\ \hline \end{array}$

8. $\begin{array}{r} 43 \\ + 15 \\ \hline \end{array}$

9. $\begin{array}{r} 18 \\ + 20 \\ \hline \end{array}$

10. $\begin{array}{r} 46 \\ + 33 \\ \hline \end{array}$

A: 79, 89, 39, 47, 58

B: 38, 58, 100, 29, 37

Winner: _____

Solve each problem. Color the sums in order on the paths to find which bee reaches the flowers first.

1. 31
    + 26

2. 50
    + 10

3. 75
    + 24

4. 66
    + 13

5. 14 + 2 + 3 = ___

6. 9 + 4 + 3 = ___

7. 39
    + 20

8. 56
    + 11

9. 9
    3
    + 5

10. 41
    3
    + 4

48	17
67	59
16	19
99	79
57	60

A   B

Winner: _____

Solve each problem. Match the sums to the numbers below. Write the letters on the lines to solve the riddle.

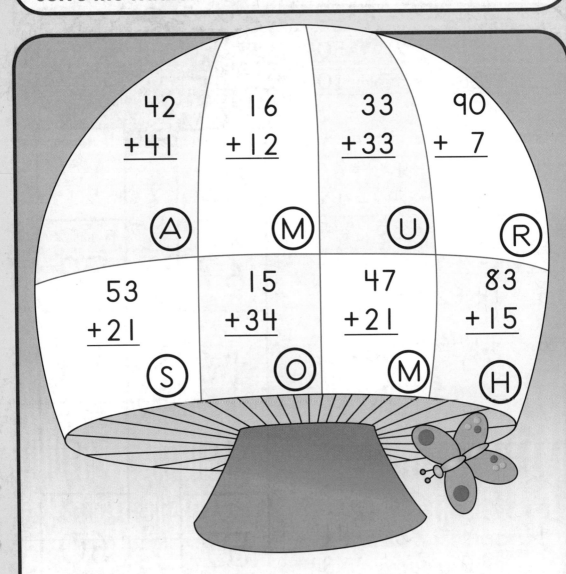

42
+41

A

16
+12

M

33
+33

U

90
+ 7

R

53
+21

S

15
+34

O

47
+21

M

83
+15

H

What kind of room can you not enter?

___ ___ ___ ___ ___ ___ ___ ___ ___
83   68   66   74   98   97   49   49   28

CD-104360

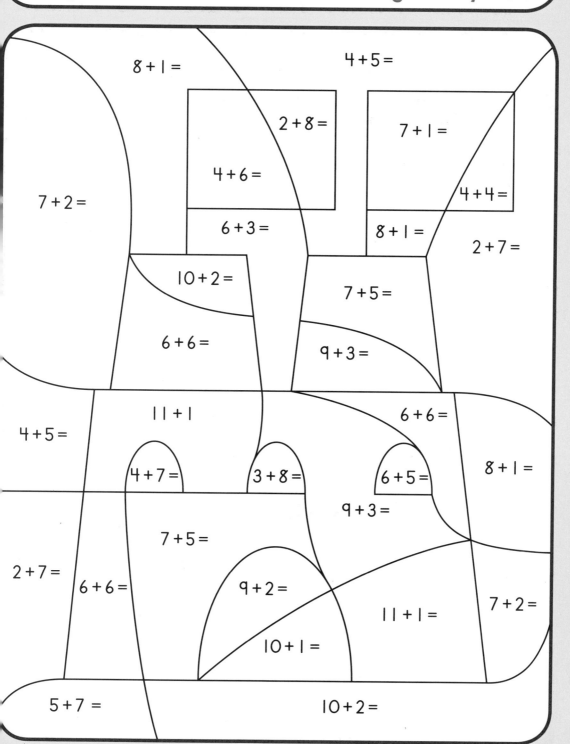

8 + 1 =

4 + 5 =

2 + 8 =

7 + 1 =

4 + 6 =

7 + 2 =

4 + 4 =

6 + 3 =

8 + 1 =

2 + 7 =

10 + 2 =

7 + 5 =

6 + 6 =

9 + 3 =

11 + 1

6 + 6 =

4 + 5 =

4 + 7 =

3 + 8 =

6 + 5 =

8 + 1 =

9 + 3 =

7 + 5 =

2 + 7 =

6 + 6 =

9 + 2 =

11 + 1 =

7 + 2 =

10 + 1 =

5 + 7 =

10 + 2 =

Solve each problem. Use the key to color the spaces and find the path that leads to the ribbon.

greater than 50 = blue   less than 50 = red

Start

$$75 - 15$$

$$99 - 23$$

$$87 - 24$$

$$42 - 11$$

$$17 - 6$$

$$82 - 10$$

$$59 - 2$$

$$54 - 24$$

$$79 - 19$$

$$67 - 5$$

$$27 - 22$$

Finish

$$68 - 34$$

$$86 - 25$$

$$91 - 60$$

$$94 - 11$$

$$63 - 12$$

Solve each problem. Put an X or an O on each difference in the tic-tac-toe board to see which letter wins. Color the winning boxes for tic-tac-toe.

$$\begin{array}{r} 94 \\ -22 \\ \hline \end{array} \textbf{X} \qquad \begin{array}{r} 16 \\ -5 \\ \hline \end{array} \textbf{X} \qquad \begin{array}{r} 37 \\ -14 \\ \hline \end{array} \textbf{O} \qquad \begin{array}{r} 85 \\ -31 \\ \hline \end{array} \textbf{O}$$

$$\begin{array}{r} 49 \\ -37 \\ \hline \end{array} \textbf{X} \qquad \begin{array}{r} 82 \\ -41 \\ \hline \end{array} \textbf{O} \qquad \begin{array}{r} 56 \\ -26 \\ \hline \end{array} \textbf{X} \qquad \begin{array}{r} 79 \\ -66 \\ \hline \end{array} \textbf{O}$$

23	72	12
62	41	54
11	30	13

Solve each problem. Match the differences to the numbers below. Write the letters on the lines to solve the riddle.

$$63 - 12$$

(N)

$$97 - 33$$

(E)

$$88 - 53$$

(A)

$$18 - 14$$

(C)

$$73 - 42$$

(E)

$$50 - 20$$

(F)

What runs around a yard without moving?

___ ___ ___ ___ ___ ___
35   30 31 51 4   64